Mik Brown's Riddle Book

Kingfisher Books

First published in this edition in 1986
by Kingfisher Books Limited
Elsley Court, 20-22 Great Titchfield Street
London W1P 7AD
A Grisewood & Dempsey Company
Material in this book originally published in 1984
in hardback in *Animal Fun: Jokes and Riddles*
Reprinted 1986

BRITISH CATALOGUING IN PUBLICATION DATA
Brown, Mik
The riddle book.
1. Riddles, Juvenile
I. Title
793.73'5   PN6371.5
ISBN 0 86272 192 X

Phototypeset by Tradespools Limited, Frome
Printed in Spain

**Where do cows go on
Saturday night?**

What do you call a bull asleep on the ground?
A bulldozer.

How do you start a flea race?
1, 2, flea, go.

Why do bees hum?
Because they don't know the words.

When did the fly fly?

What lies down a hundred feet in the air?
A centipede.

What's white outside, green inside and hops?
A frog sandwich.

Where do tadpoles
turn into frogs?

What's red and flies
and wobbles at the
same time?

A jellycopter.

A giraffe with a sore throat.

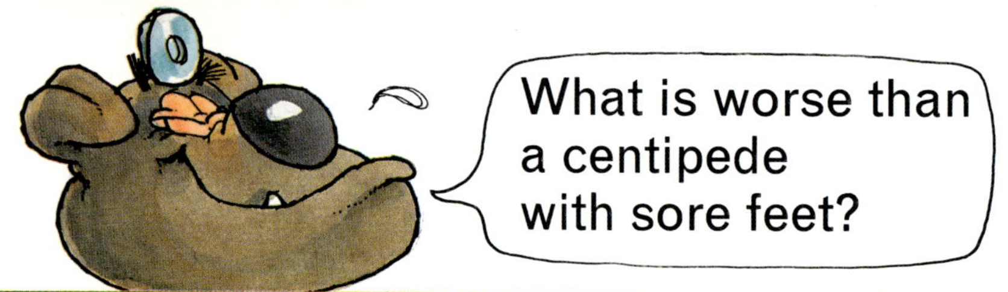

PATIENT: "Doctor, doctor, I've got a terrible sore throat."
DOCTOR: "Go over to the window and stick your tongue out."
PATIENT: "Will that help my throat?"
DOCTOR: "No, I just don't like the man next door."

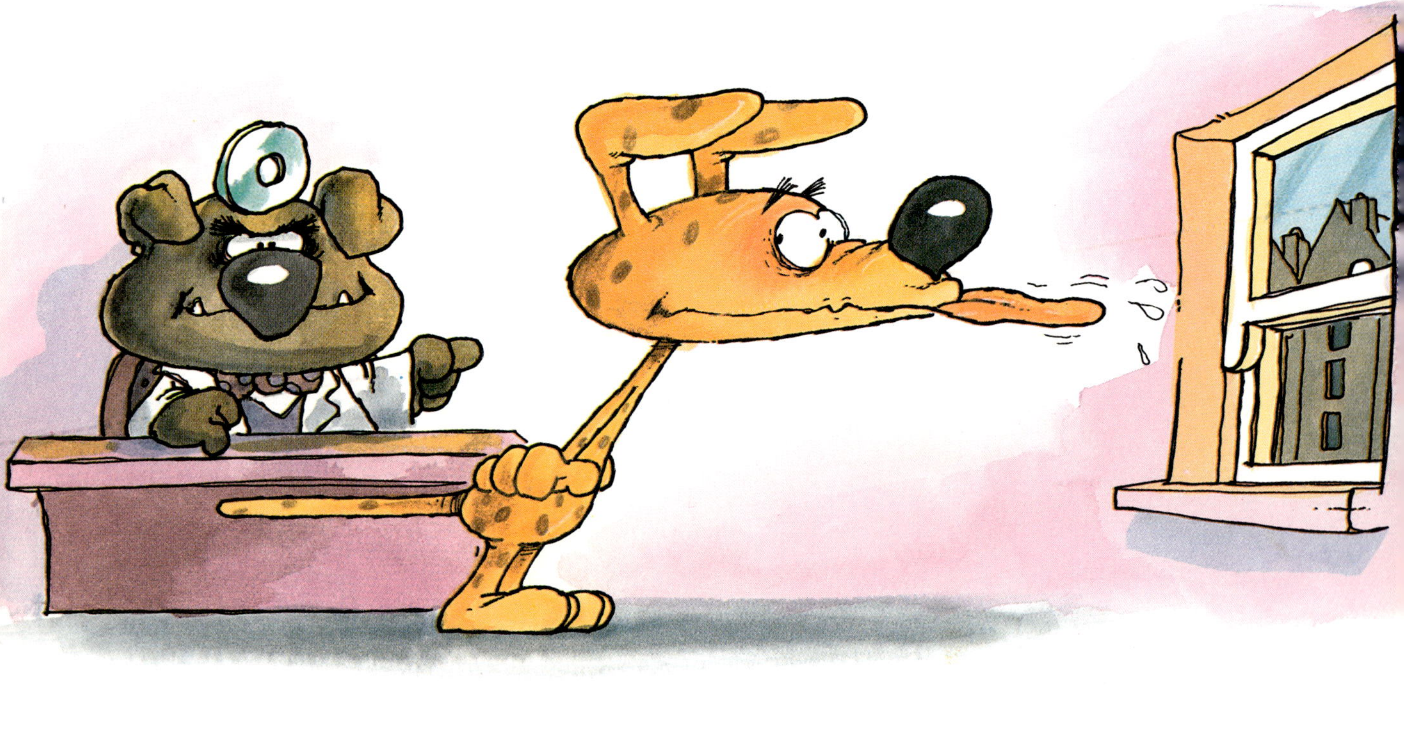

FREDA: "Will I be able to read with these glasses?"
FRED: "You certainly will."
FREDA: "That's good, I couldn't before."

What do mice do in the daytime?
Mousework.

What's white, has four legs and a trunk?
A mouse going on holiday.

How can you tell
one cat from
another?

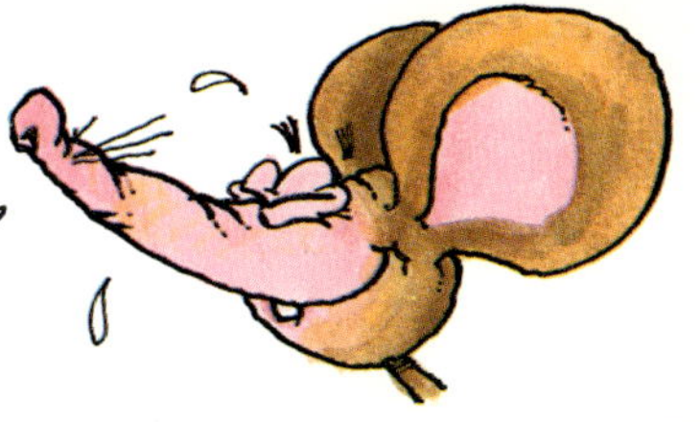

What's grey, has four legs and
weighs one-and-a-half pounds?

A fat mouse.

What's brown, has four legs
and a trunk?

*A mouse coming back
from holiday.*

Time to fix the fence.

What do you call an elephant that flies?

A jumbo jet.

**How do you know there's an elephant
under your bed?**

When your nose touches the ceiling.

Why shouldn't you tell a secret to a pig?

Because he's a squealer.

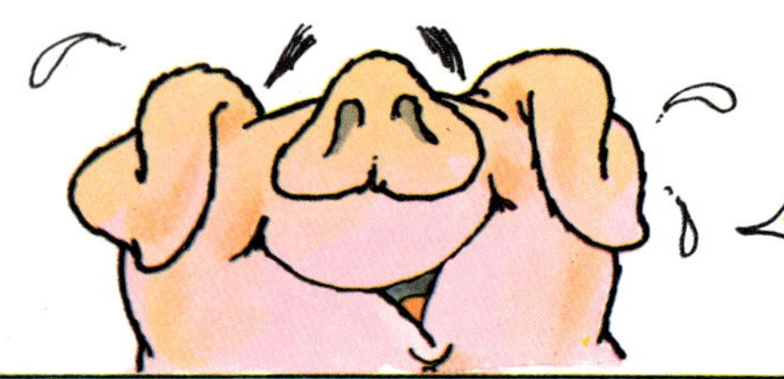

Why is getting up in the morning like a pig's tail?

Because it's twirly. (Too early.)

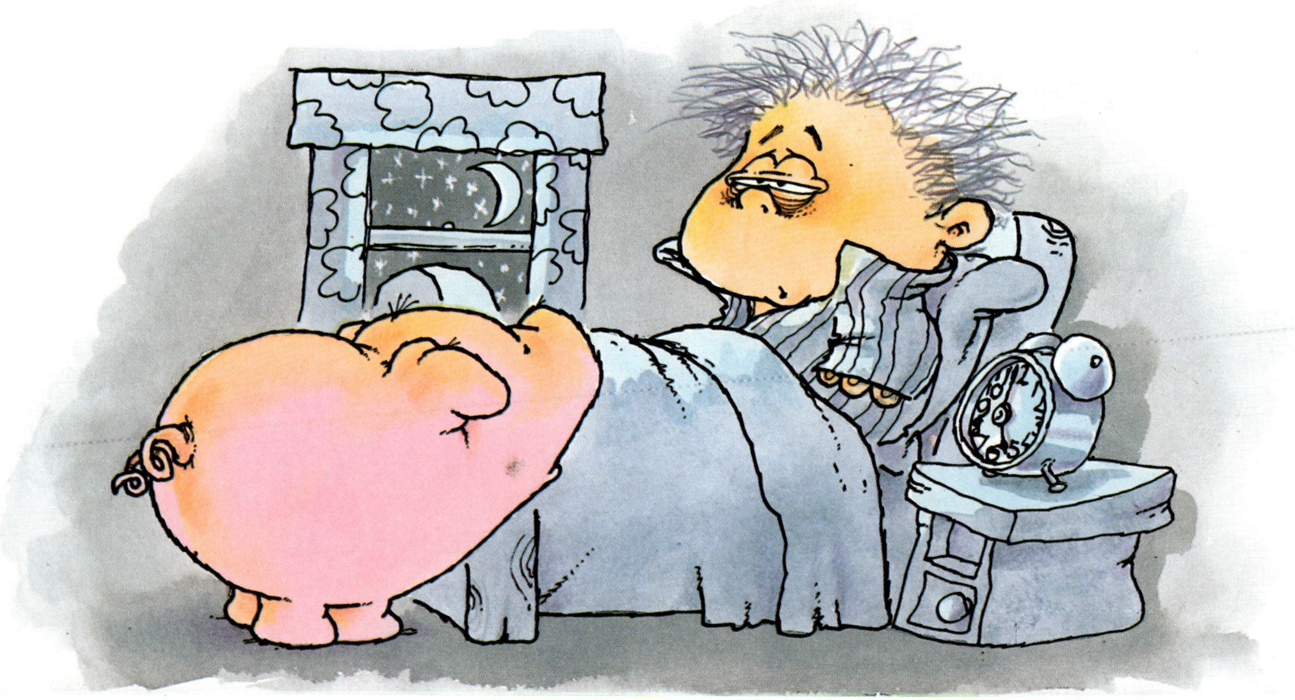

What kind of tie does a pig wear?
A pigsty.

What do you give
a sick pig?
Oinkment.

What do you get if
you pour hot water
down a rabbit hole?

Hot-cross-bunnies.

How do you tell a rabbit
from a gorilla?

*A rabbit doesn't
look like a gorilla.*

What is a twip?

A can of people.

TEACHER: "You should have been here at 9 o'clock."
PUPIL: "Why, what happened?"

Why are goldfish red?
The water makes them rusty.

What's yellow and
highly dangerous?

Shark-infested custard.

What happened to the lion who slept with his head under the pillow?

The fairies took all his teeth away.

Which animal should
you never trust?

What's yellow and black
with red spots?

A leopard with measles.

If athletes get athlete's foot,
what do astronauts get?

Missile toe.

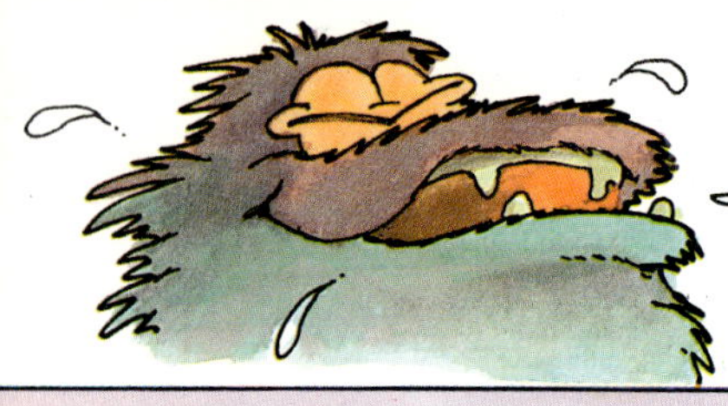

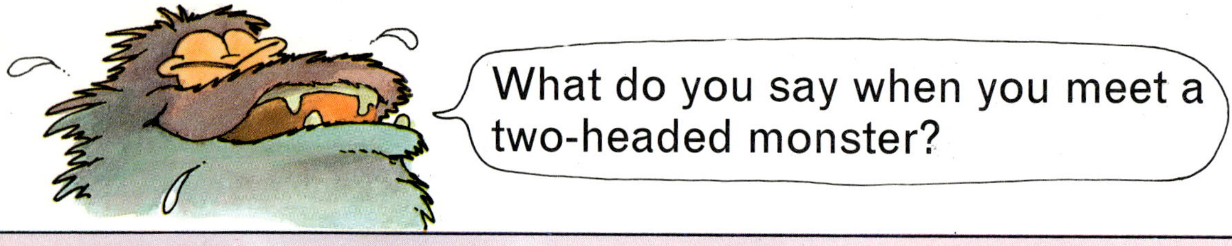

"Hello, hello."

What's the difference between a huge, smelly, ugly monster and a sweet?

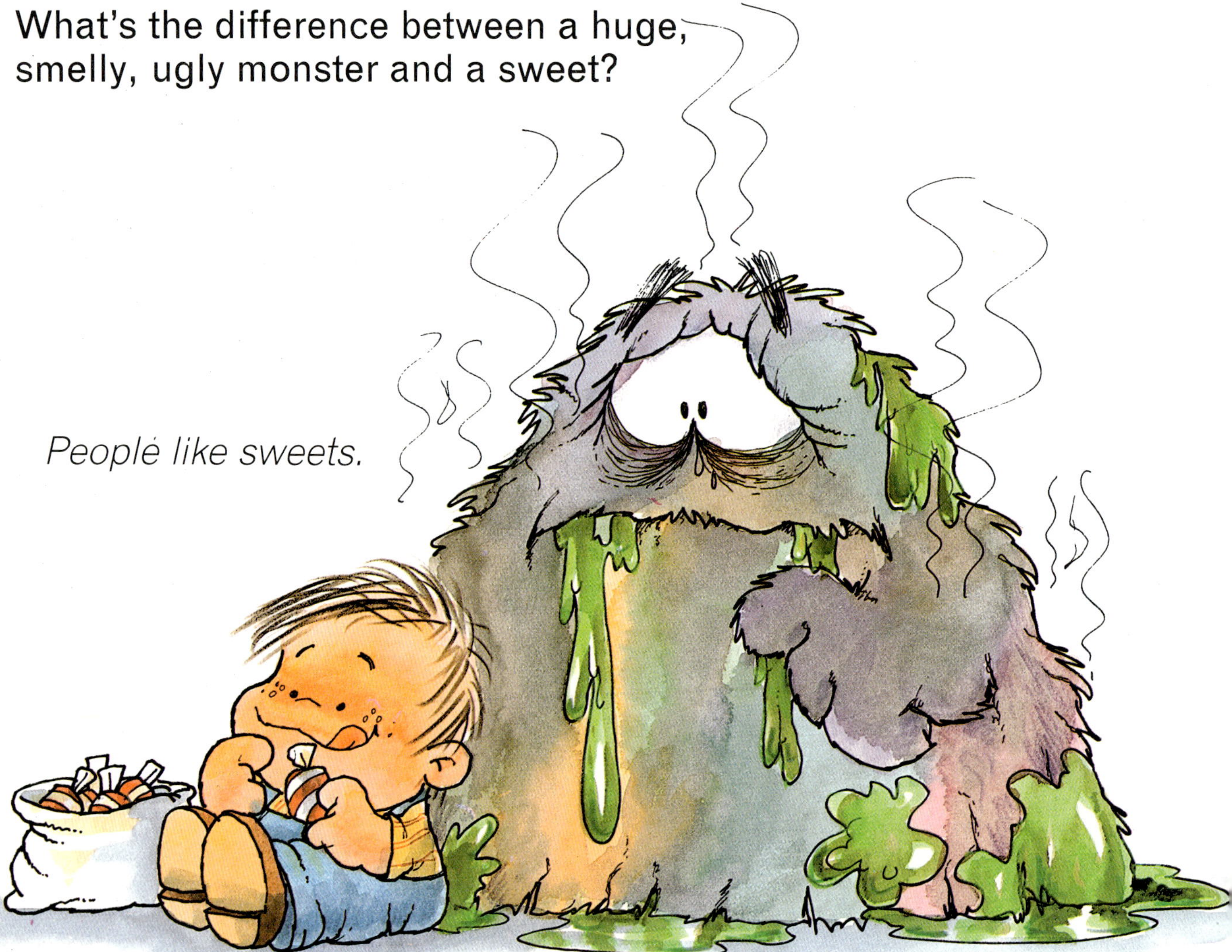

People like sweets.

What has a purple-spotted body, hairy legs and big eyes on stalks?

I don't know, but there's one crawling up your leg.

A kitten.

Why do cats have furry coats?

Because they look silly in plastic macs.

When is it bad luck to be followed by a black cat?
When you're a mouse.

What do angry mice send each other at Christmas?
Cross-mouse cards.

What should you do if you find a snake in your bed?
Sleep on the wardrobe.

What snake is good at sums?

FIRST SNAKE: "Are we supposed
to be poisonous?"
SECOND SNAKE: "Why?"
FIRST SNAKE: "Because I've just
bitten my lip."

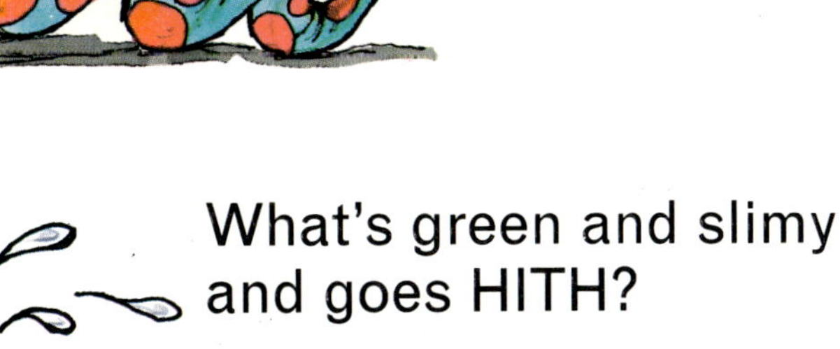

What's green and slimy
and goes HITH?

A snake with a lisp.

How does a sparrow with engine trouble manage to land safely?
With its sparrowchute.

Why do birds fly south in the winter?
Because it's too far to walk.

Why don't ducks tell jokes when they're flying?

What's black and white and red all over?

A sunburnt penguin.

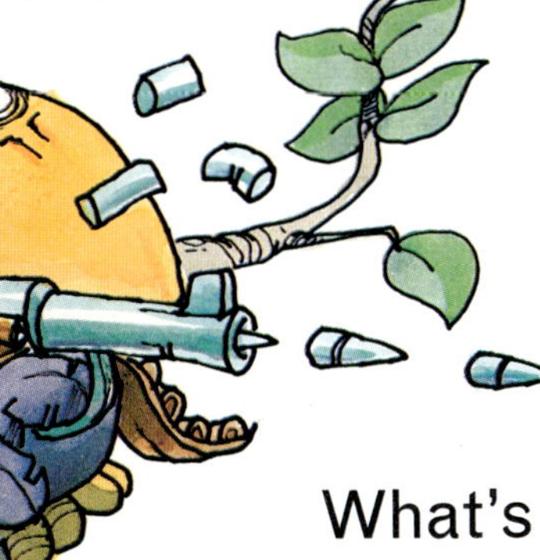

What's black and shiny, lives in trees and is very dangerous?

A crow with a machine gun.

What do baby apes sleep in?
Apricots.

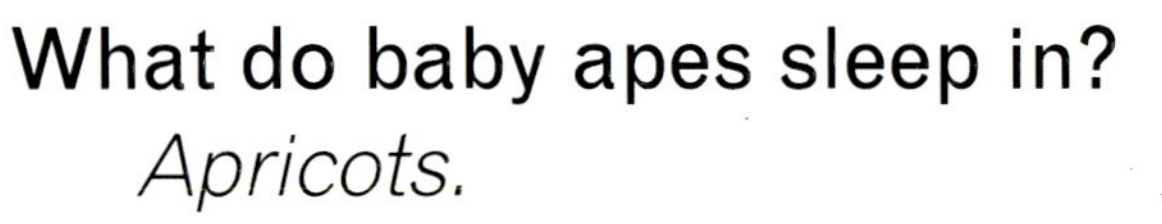

How did the monkey make toast?
He put it under the gorilla.

Why does a monkey
scratch himself?

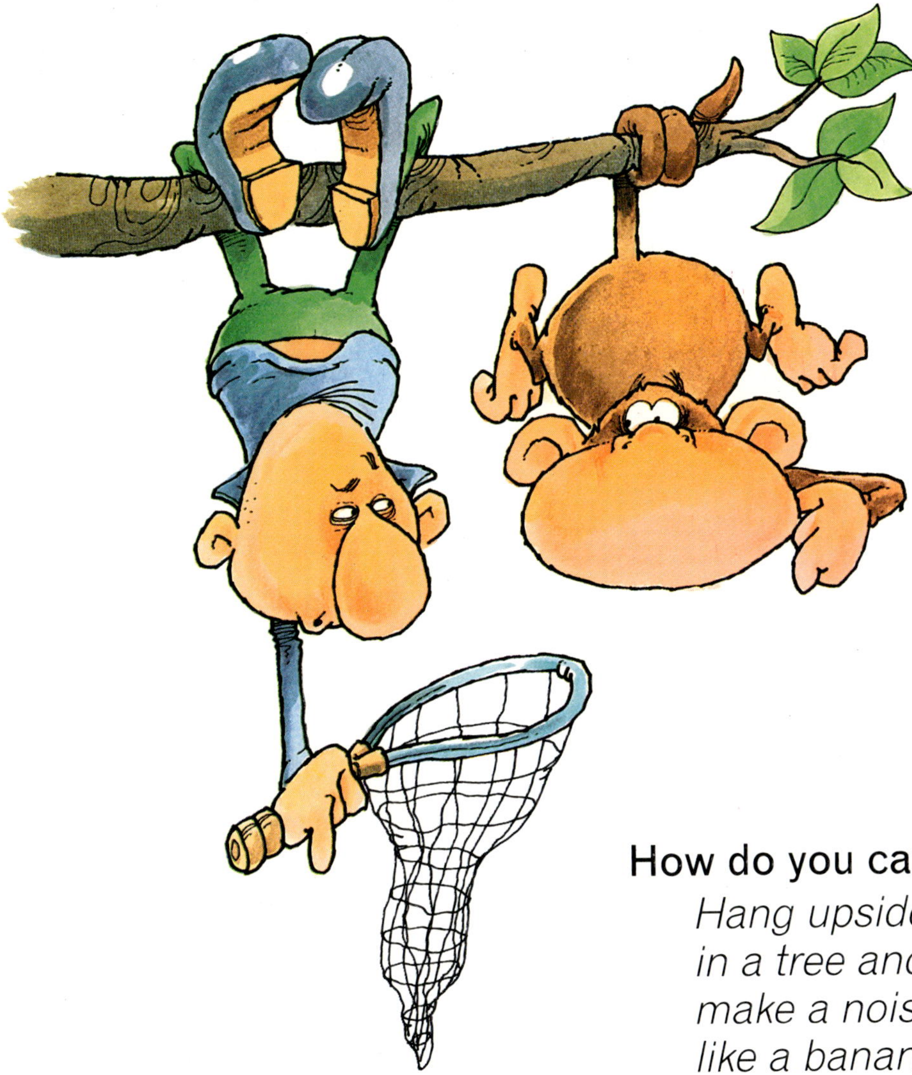

How do you catch a monkey?

*Hang upside down
in a tree and
make a noise
like a banana.*

In a moo-seum.

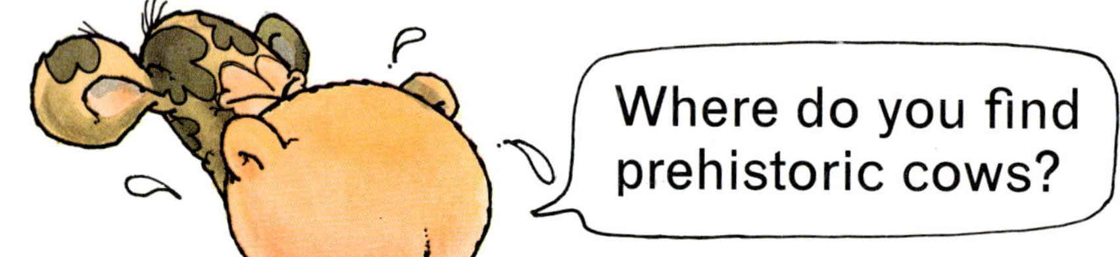

Which cows have the shortest legs?

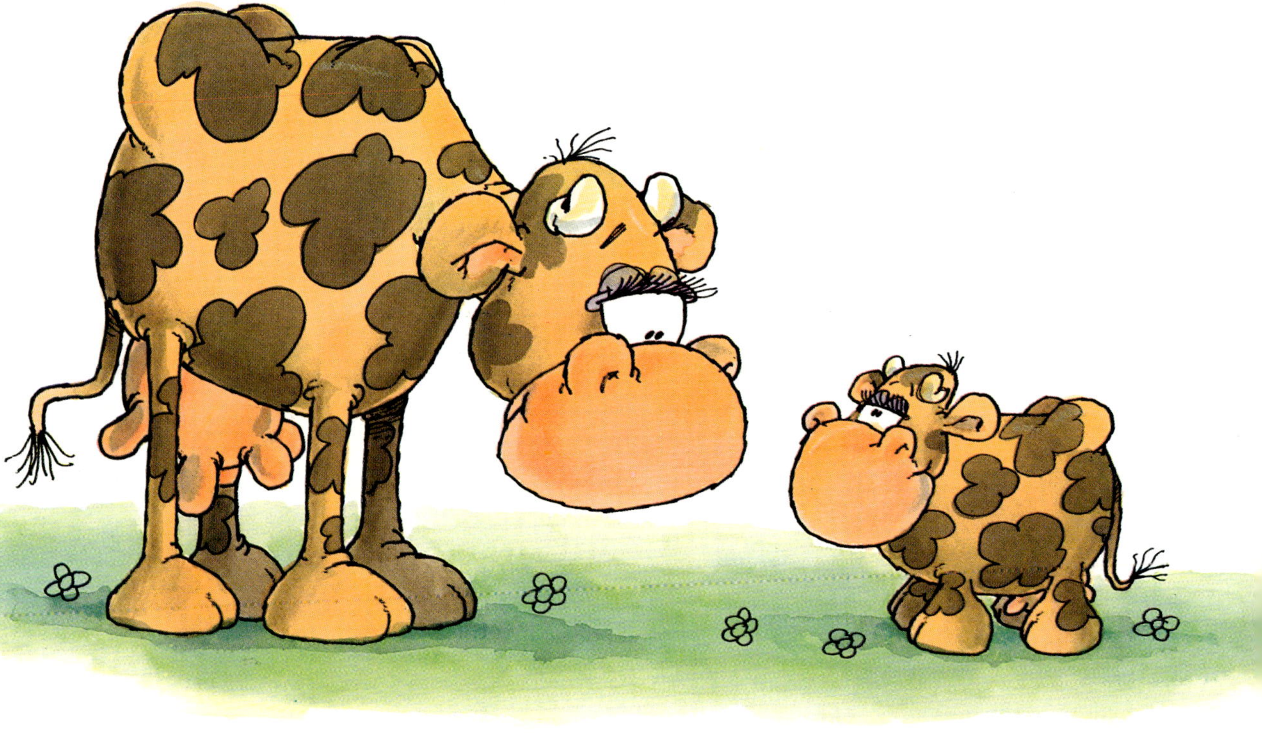

The smallest ones.